Where Are the Galapagos Islands?

by Megan Stine

illustrated by John Hinderliter

Penguin Workshop
An Imprint of Penguin Random House

For Daryl—MS

For Carson and Bryce.
Books are full of adventure—JH

PENGUIN WORKSHOP
Penguin Young Readers Group
An Imprint of Penguin Random House LLC

Library of Congress Control Number: 2017010005

ISBN 9780451533876 (paperback)   10 9 8 7 6 5 4
ISBN 9780451533890 (library binding)   10 9 8 7 6 5 4 3 2 1

Contents

Where Are the Galapagos Islands? 1

The Islands Are Born 8

Pirates and Whales 14

Darwin Arrives 24

Meet the Islands 43

The Weirdest Birds in the World 62

Land Animals in a Water World 76

The Human Threat 87

Protecting the Islands 98

Timelines 106

Bibliography 108

Where Are the Galapagos Islands?

It was a hot, dry day in March. The year was 1535. Brother Tomas, the bishop of Panama, was on board a ship sailing from Panama to Peru. He had been sent by King Charles I of Spain to settle problems in Peru. (Spain owned Peru at that time.) The bishop thought there was enough food and water for the trip, but he was wrong. After seven days at sea, the wind suddenly died down. His ship was stranded in the Pacific Ocean. There was no way other than wind to make the ship move—motors didn't exist yet. He could do nothing but wait until the wind picked up again to fill the sails.

For several days, the ship drifted on the ocean currents. The men on board were so thirsty, they thought they might die. They couldn't drink the salty seawater—it would have killed them. Finally, on March 10, they spotted land. Islands! They had drifted toward an amazing place that wasn't on any map. No one lived on these islands. No one even knew these islands existed!

Quickly they anchored the boat. The bishop and crew went ashore, hoping to find food and water.

What they saw seemed like a cross between heaven and hell on earth.

The islands were alive with animals the sailors had never seen before. There were giant tortoises big enough for a man to ride! There were iguanas that knew how to dive and swim! There were hundreds of strange birds that weren't afraid of people. They would perch on a sailor's head, or hop right onto his hand. Some birds had bright blue feet and walked in a funny waddle.

But there was no freshwater to be found. When the bishop's men dug a well, the water that came out was saltier than the ocean. And much of the landscape was so rocky and harsh, plants could not grow. On some islands, the land was covered with solid black lava—sharp to the touch and difficult to walk on. The bishop said it looked like "God had showered stones."

All the men had to eat were sour prickly cactuses. They sucked the liquid out of them to survive. The bishop and his men searched several of the islands, but two men and some horses died of thirst before they could find any freshwater to drink. When a breeze finally blew in after two days, they quickly reboarded the ship and sailed away.

The bishop didn't give a name to the islands. But he did write to the king of Spain, describing this otherworldly place. He mentioned the giant tortoises, called *galápagos* in Spanish. The islands appeared on a map a few years later with that name—Galapagos.

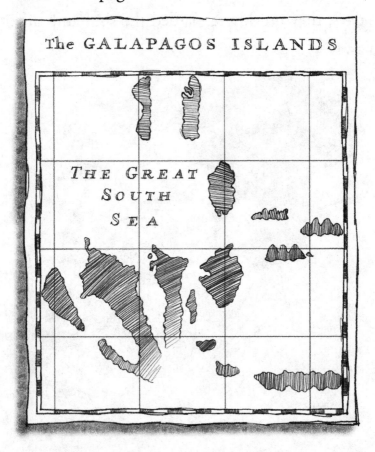

The GALAPAGOS ISLANDS

THE GREAT SOUTH SEA

It would take another 150 years before anyone visited again or wrote about this strange, magical place. And it would be exactly three hundred years till the most famous visitor of all arrived—a young scientist named Charles Darwin. When he landed on the Galapagos and saw the creatures there, he came up with an idea about how all forms of life change over time. His big idea— called evolution—changed the world. Because of Darwin, the Galapagos Islands became the famous place they are today.

CHAPTER 1
The Islands Are Born

Millions of years ago, a volcano began erupting underwater in the Pacific Ocean. It was six hundred miles off the west coast of South America, near the equator. Hot lava—melted rock—shot up through a gap in the earth's crust at the bottom of the sea. As the lava cooled, it formed a mountain—an underwater mountain! Each time the volcano erupted, more lava came up and the underwater mountain grew taller. Eventually, it was so tall that its top rose above the water.

A new island had been born.

Over time—thousands of years—that island moved to the east. Then, when the volcano erupted again, another island was created where the first one had been. The same thing happened over and over. Each time a new island was created, it ended up moving east. After millions of years, there was a whole string of islands. As one scientist said, the islands seemed to be moving on a conveyor belt, the kind of belt that carries your groceries in a supermarket.

Tectonic Plates—How Islands Can Move

Strange as it may seem, all the land masses on earth are always moving. They move because the earth's crust—the outermost layer of the planet—is made up of a number of separate pieces. These pieces are called tectonic plates. Imagine that the earth is like an orange. If you remove the peel and cut it into pieces, and then put them back together, they would still cover the orange—but not in one piece anymore. That's how the earth's crust is. It's made up of separate pieces. They can move because they aren't attached to

North American Plate

Juan de Fuca Plate

Caribbean Plate

Cocos Plate

Pacific Plate

Nazca Plate

Juan Fernández Plate

Easter Plate

Scotia Plate

one another, and because they're floating on the soft liquid inside the earth, which is melted rock.

The Galapagos Islands move two to three inches every year. The first island has moved more than one hundred miles since it was born 3.5 million years ago.

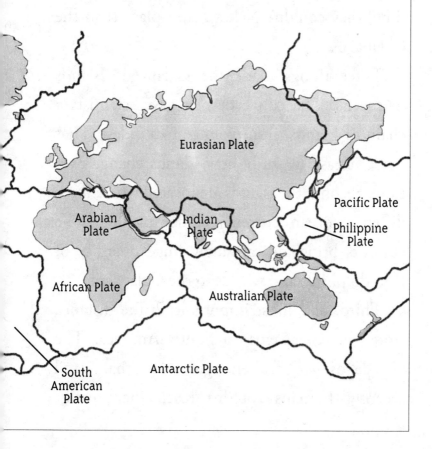

At first there was no life on the Galapagos Islands. They were just barren rock. But over time, that changed. The islands were in a spot that turned out to be perfect for life-forms to develop. In fact, if scientists wanted to set up an experiment to see how life changes over time, they couldn't pick a better place than the Galapagos.

Three things made the Galapagos Islands so special. The conveyor belt gave scientists a chain of islands, from youngest to oldest. That made it easy to study how islands change over time. Second, the islands are located where three different ocean currents come together. The currents bring an amazingly huge quantity of fish, dolphins, and whales to the Galapagos.

Third, and most important, is the distance from the Galapagos to South America. The Galapagos are far enough away that until recently, humans couldn't reach them easily.

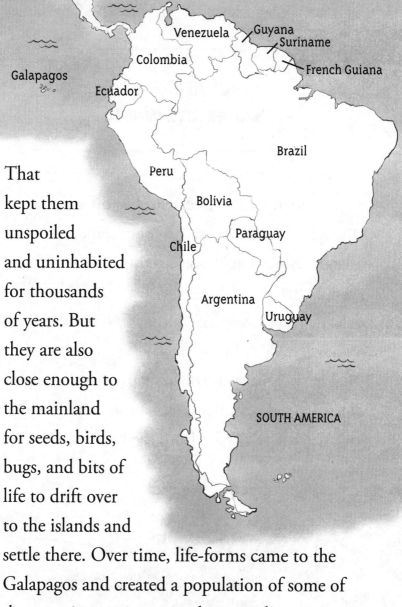

Galapagos

Venezuela

Guyana

Suriname

Colombia

French Guiana

Ecuador

Peru

Brazil

Bolivia

Paraguay

Chile

Argentina

Uruguay

SOUTH AMERICA

That
kept them
unspoiled
and uninhabited
for thousands
of years. But
they are also
close enough to
the mainland
for seeds, birds,
bugs, and bits of
life to drift over
to the islands and
settle there. Over time, life-forms came to the
Galapagos and created a population of some of
the most interesting animals on earth.

CHAPTER 2
Pirates and Whales

For many years after the bishop of Panama discovered Galapagos, no one came near the islands. No one had ever lived there, and no one wanted to.

Then, in the 1680s, new visitors arrived. Pirates!

The oceans were filled with pirate ships in those days. They attacked Spanish ships carrying treasure back to Spain from the New World.

Most pirates patrolled the waters in the Caribbean near lands that Spain had claimed. But some sailed all the way around the southern tip of South America—Cape Horn. From there, they went north along the west coast of South America. It was only a matter of time before some pirates decided to check out the Galapagos that were showing up on new maps. The islands became a pirate hideout. Sometimes pirates buried treasure there. Years later, people found coins, called pieces of eight, in the sand.

One of the earliest visitors was William Dampier. Dampier wasn't a true pirate, since he worked for the British Navy. He was a privateer. But his job was the same as a pirate's— to attack Spanish ships and take all

William Dampier

their treasure. The only difference was that pirates kept everything. Privateers gave the treasure to their home country.

On one trip, Dampier's crew captured a ship and took the Spanish prisoners to the Galapagos. Always interested in nature, Dampier kept notes in a journal, writing down a full description of the islands. His notes were published. So were notes and maps from other sea captains at the time.

Pretty soon, the word got around that the Galapagos Islands had lots to offer—fish, huge tortoises so big that one could feed an entire crew, and one more thing that everyone wanted. Whales!

Whale oil, from the blubber of whales, was an important source of energy in those days. Many lamps were lighted with whale oil. It was also used to make soap and to grease machines.

The whaling industry in the Atlantic Ocean was a big business. So big that by the 1790s, the whale population in the Atlantic was dying out. So when word spread about all the whales near Galapagos, that was where the whaling ships went. On arrival in the Galapagos, the sailors found whales gathered by the dozens—sperm whales, orcas, blue whales, and humpbacks. Before long, whales had been killed off in huge numbers.

Moby-Dick

One famous American whaler who sailed to the Galapagos was named Herman Melville. In 1841, as a young man, he joined a whaling ship and sailed around the world. When he grew older, he wrote a famous novel called *Moby-Dick*. It is all about a sea captain named Ahab who is trying to catch an enormous whale in the Pacific Ocean that has bitten off part of his leg. Melville also published a book of short stories about his visits to the Galapagos.

Captain Ahab

The whalers and pirates who arrived at Galapagos were often hungry. They captured huge numbers of giant tortoises that roamed the islands. The tortoises weighed up to 550 pounds each—big enough to feed a crew for days or weeks. They were easy to catch or kill, since they moved so slowly. And they were delicious. Tortoise meat was a sweet delicacy that the sailors never got tired of eating.

The tortoises could live for months in the hold of a ship, so they provided fresh food for the sailors to eat while at sea. Fat from the tortoises was tasty, too. It was used instead of butter.

Thousands of tortoises were taken during the pirate and whaling years. Sailors often caught twenty or thirty a day. It was heavy work, though. Sometimes it took six or more men to lift one tortoise. Ships sailed away with dozens or even hundreds of animals aboard. After two hundred years, more than one hundred thousand tortoises had been captured and killed.

But luckily there were still plenty of tortoises around when Charles Darwin came to visit. The tortoises turned out to be one of the clues that helped Darwin solve the puzzle of how creatures change over time.

Charles Darwin

CHAPTER 3
Darwin Arrives

In 1831, Charles Darwin was a student in England who loved nature and science. As a child, he had loved collecting things—stones and birds' eggs. In college, he studied plants and collected beetles. But what should he do for a career? One of Darwin's professors suggested he go with Captain Robert FitzRoy on a trip around the world. This sounded like a wonderful adventure to Darwin. So at the age of twenty-two, he boarded a ship

Captain FitzRoy

called the HMS *Beagle*.
He knew the trip would take
a long time—but he had no idea he
would be leaving England for five years!

His plan was to collect samples of plants and
animals everywhere he went. He was especially
excited to visit Galapagos. He had read about
the islands in a book by an American sea captain
named Benjamin Morrell.

Morrell's ship had sailed from New York to Galapagos in February 1825. A few days after he arrived, a volcano erupted. It sent fire and ash into the night sky—so much that it looked like the whole island was on fire. As rivers of molten lava ran down the mountain and into the sea, the seawater became hot—more than one hundred degrees! The ocean was so hot, the glue that held wooden pieces of the ship together began to melt. The air was so hot, sailors couldn't breathe! And they couldn't sail away from the islands, because there was no breeze.

Finally the wind picked up. Morrell managed to escape the fiery island and wrote down his experiences. Darwin hoped that he, too, would see the same volcano erupt when he reached the Galapagos.

Instead, when the *Beagle* reached the area, Darwin found the islands very still and calm. Parts of some islands were nothing but solid black ribbons of lava. Other islands were thick with strange trees called mangroves.

The Islands of the Archipelago

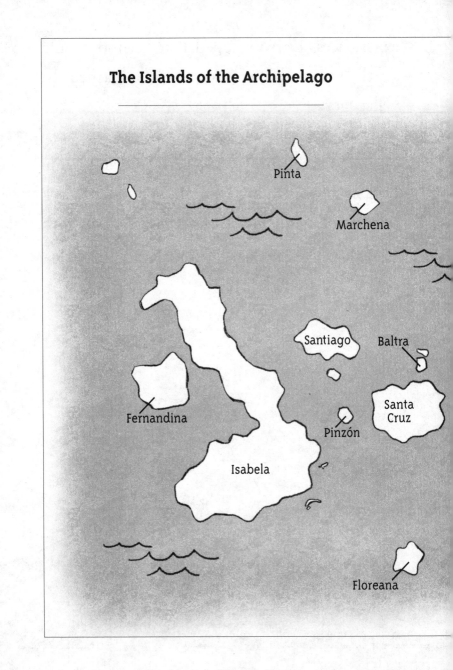

The Galapagos is a chain of islands called an archipelago. There are thirteen main islands, and lots of smaller ones, which are called islets or just plain rocks.

Genovesa

When the *Beagle* arrived in 1835, Darwin first went ashore on San Cristóbal. A few days later, they sailed on to Floreana, then Isabela and Santiago. At the time, Floreana was the only inhabited island. Humans had been living there for only a few years. Today four of the islands are inhabited—Isabela, Santa Cruz, San Cristóbal, and Floreana.

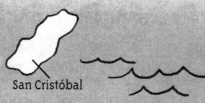
San Cristóbal

Santa Fé

Española

At first, Darwin was more interested in the rocks than the plants and animals. He hoped to figure out how volcanoes worked. By studying different sections of lava from different volcanoes, Darwin realized that the Galapagos Islands were fairly new compared to the rest of the land on earth. He also guessed or suspected that the islands had been underwater at some point. Was this a clue to how land on earth was formed? Did it prove that the islands at one time had nothing growing or living on them? Darwin had more questions than answers at first.

Pretty soon, though, Darwin began to study the wildlife, not just the rocks and plants. The creatures on the island were so amazing, especially the iguanas, birds, and tortoises. He even rode on a tortoise. He measured it. It was five feet long. Then he flipped it over, to see if it could manage to get back on its own feet. It did.

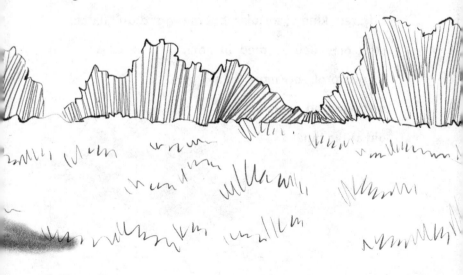

Lonesome George

Giant tortoises are almost like the mascots of the Galapagos Islands. Each island has a different kind. In the past, there were fourteen different species. (A *species* is a type of plant, animal, or other living thing.) Now four of them are extinct. That means those four species died out—there are none left. The last remaining tortoise on Pinta Island was called Lonesome George. He was the only living example of his kind. Scientists tried to mate him with a slightly different kind of tortoise, but the eggs didn't hatch. Lonesome George died in 2012. He was probably more than one hundred years old at the time.

Darwin and Captain FitzRoy spent a few days on each of four islands. It was then that Darwin noticed all tortoises didn't have the same kinds of shells. Some of them had shells like an upside-down bowl. But others had a shell that curved up near the animal's head— like a Spanish saddle.

The curve in the saddleback shells allowed the tortoise to lift its head up higher and eat leaves from taller plants. The tortoises with bowl-shaped shells could eat only plants that were low to the ground.

A man who lived on Floreana told Darwin that he could identify which island a tortoise came from just by looking at its shell. In other words, each island had tortoises that were unique to that particular place. Depending on where they lived, tortoises had changed over time. Darwin didn't realize right away how important this information was. He didn't even collect or save any of the giant tortoise shells.

He started collecting other specimens, though. In those days, it was common for scientists to kill birds and other animals so they could study them later. Darwin collected birds, beetles—all sorts of creatures and plants. He packed away as many as he had room for on the ship. Later, they would be donated to a museum.

Darwin collected lots of birds that all turned out to be finches—thirteen different kinds. But he didn't write down one important fact. He didn't label which island each bird came from. He hadn't yet begun to figure out how the Galapagos Islands worked—that each island had a different environment that caused the life-forms to change over time.

But a few years later, he began to think about the finches he had collected. Fortunately, Captain FitzRoy had collected some finches himself—and his were labeled correctly. Captain FitzRoy helped to figure out which islands Darwin's finches came from. Then Darwin thought more about what the man on Floreana had said about the tortoise shells. Slowly, he started to put the pieces of the puzzle together, and came up with his groundbreaking theory about evolution. A theory is a big idea that explains facts or events. Darwin's theory of evolution explained how and why species changed over time.

Before Darwin's time, most people believed that all living species had been created in a short period of time, about five or six thousand years ago. They also believed that once a species was created, it never changed.

Darwin thought differently because of what he observed in the natural world and what he saw on his trip to the Galapagos.

First, he noticed that not all baby animals survive long enough to have babies of their own. There just isn't enough food for all the babies, so only some will survive and reproduce.

Second, he noticed that some baby animals are born with traits that are different from their parents'. If the different trait is useful or helpful for survival, that baby will be more likely to live longer and pass that trait on to its own offspring. Over time, a whole new species may evolve, with all the traits useful for survival.

On Galapagos, for example, Darwin noticed that some finches had large, rounded beaks. They lived on islands with lots of seeds. Big beaks are good for breaking seeds from plants—so if a baby finch was born on an island with a lot of seeds, that was a useful trait to have. Those babies were likely to survive and pass that trait on to their offspring.

But other islands had very few seeds. So having a big, round beak wouldn't help finches survive. And indeed, Darwin saw that finches on these islands had different beaks—long, sharp beaks. These beaks could pull tiny insects from trees so the finches could eat them.

In other words, Darwin realized that the birds on Galapagos changed (or evolved) differently on each island, because each island offered different kinds of food.

Darwin called this process of passing on useful traits "natural selection," because the species that were best suited to survive were selected naturally.

In 1859, Darwin published a book called *On the Origin of Species.* In it, he explained his big theory about evolution. It took the scientific world by storm.

The Galapagos had been the key to Darwin's understanding of evolution. He realized that the first birds, plants, and animals on the islands had probably come from South America, just six hundred miles away. On arrival, all the finches, for example, were the same as the finches in South America. But over time, through natural selection, they evolved into different species that were suited to the environment on each of the islands.

Tortoises followed the same pattern as finches. Over time, tortoises on islands with very tall plants had evolved into creatures whose shells let them stretch their necks and reach higher leaves to eat. Over millions of years, these tortoises came to have saddleback shells. But tortoises that lived on islands with a lot of low-growing plants could find food, even with their bowl-shaped shells. There was no need for them to evolve.

Over and over, Darwin saw how the natural environment had played a part in the evolution of species. Exploring the Galapagos Islands led to the origin of his very bold new theory. He called the Galapagos "the origin of all my views."

CHAPTER 4
Meet the Islands

Each of the Galapagos Islands has its own special environment. But all the islands have one thing in common. They are located right on or near the equator—the imaginary belt that circles the very middle of the globe. The seasons never change on the equator—it's always summer!

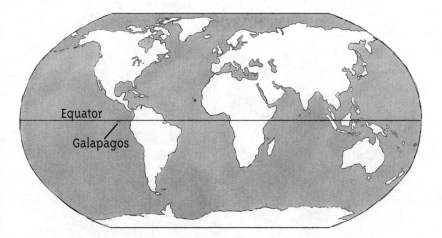

Equator

Galapagos

The youngest island is Fernandina. The volcano that created it—the one that Captain Morrell saw exploding—is still active. It erupted in 2009, killing animals there. It will probably erupt again before the year 2025. Luckily, no people are killed when it explodes, because no humans live on this rocky, remote island. But there is lots of wildlife. It is home to marine iguanas—iguanas that dive into the sea from the rocky cliffs. It is also a favorite spot for sea lions, penguins, pelicans, and a bird called the flightless cormorant.

Fernandina is the most unspoiled of all the Galapagos Islands. There are almost no plants on Fernandina, except for mangrove trees that grow on the coast in the saltwater. It's almost impossible for anything to grow on the rocky surface created by an active volcano, because there is no soil.

Isabela is the next island to the east. Shaped like a seahorse, Isabela is the largest island in the Galapagos—sixty-two miles long. Only four of the thirteen main islands have people living on them, and Isabela is one.

At the southern tip of the island, there's a small village where most of the people on Isabela live. There are only about two thousand people on the whole island.

Although it's the second-youngest island, Isabela has existed long enough for the rocky landscape to erode, which allowed soil to form. Lush plants now cover parts of the island. But Isabela itself was created from six erupting volcanoes, and most of them are still active. The largest volcano, called Sierra Negra, erupted for eight days in 2005. Sometimes, the volcanoes erupt for months at a time!

Isabela has more giant tortoises than any of the other islands—about five thousand. It is also home to one of the strangest birds in the world— the blue-footed booby. The waters near Isabela are a perfect place to see whales, and the lagoons are filled with pink flamingos.

In addition to Isabela, the three other islands that have humans living on them are Santa Cruz, San Cristóbal, and Floreana. But even these islands are mostly uninhabited. Nearly all of the Galapagos Islands—97 percent—is set aside as a national park.

Santa Cruz has the largest population. About twelve thousand people live there. It has a good-size town with restaurants, hotels, shops, a hospital, and banks.

Tourists often visit Santa Cruz to shop and dine. They also come to see the Charles Darwin Research Station, where scientists study the islands' life-forms. There are farms, beaches, wildlife parks, and volcanic craters on Santa Cruz. The island is also known as a beautiful place to watch flamingos.

San Cristóbal is the oldest of the islands, and the farthest east. This was where Darwin first arrived in 1835, with Captain FitzRoy. It is also the capital of Galapagos. Police and government offices are there, as well as a modern airport. Sea lions, tortoises, dolphins, and unusual birds are all at home on this island as well.

Floreana is one of the smaller islands, and it has a very small population. As one of the oldest islands, it has more plants and animal species than the younger islands. At one time, Floreana was a pirate hangout. Pirate treasure has been found there.

Years ago, when pirates and whalers visited Floreana, they came up with a system for sending mail back home. They set up a wooden barrel where anyone could leave mail. They called it Post Office Bay. Anyone who came along could pick up the letters and deliver them when they got back home. Sometimes it took a year or more for a letter to arrive. Today, the barrel still exists on Floreana. People still leave postcards there for others to deliver!

Who Owns the Galapagos?

Spanish sailors were the first people to arrive in the Galapagos. But Spain didn't claim the islands for themselves. So in 1832, Ecuador sent a man named General Jose Villamil to create a small settlement and claim the islands for Ecuador. He held a ceremony on February 12 to mark the occasion.

Villamil decided to settle Floreana first. Very few people wanted to move to a deserted island in the Pacific Ocean, so Villamil took some scruffy men with him. Some of the men were convicted criminals. Life was very hard. For a while, the islands became a penal colony—a place for people who were sent to prison.

General Jose Villamil

Galapagos is still ruled by Ecuador today. Every year, they celebrate "Galapagos Day" on February 12. That also happens to be Darwin's birthday!

The rest of the Galapagos Islands are uninhabited—no humans live there. The other main islands are: Santiago, Española, Pinta, Genovesa, Marchena, Santa Fé, Pinzón, and Baltra. All of these islands, except for Baltra, are known as amazing habitats for wonderful, unusual birds and animals. The coastal waters are also filled with spectacular fish, dolphins, sharks, and whales. Many of the islands host species that live nowhere else on earth. For instance, the Galapagos pink iguana lives only on Isabela Island.

Pink iguana

And the Floreana mockingbird is so rare, it can't even be found on Floreana anymore. There are only a few remaining birds, living on two tiny islets nearby.

Floreana mockingbird

Baltra is the oddball island. It is small and very flat, with fewer interesting species than the other islands. During World War II, the United States was fighting against Japan. The US needed an air force base in the Pacific Ocean—a place where planes could take off and land. With permission from Ecuador, a runway was built on Baltra.

During the war, President Franklin D. Roosevelt's wife, Eleanor, came to visit. She wanted to cheer up the troops who were stationed there—but she didn't find the island very cheerful! She called it "one of the most discouraging spots in the world."

Eleanor Roosevelt

After the war, the runway remained. It let private planes bring visitors to the Galapagos. Slowly but surely, people began to discover these hidden gems of wonderful wildlife. People wanted to see the giant tortoises, blue-footed boobies, and tiny penguins—the only penguins that live north of the equator. They wanted to watch the iguanas diving from the cliffs into the ocean. Tourists were eager to see the flightless bird that had developed here—and nowhere else on earth.

Habitats of the Galapagos

It's always warm on the Galapagos—seventy-five to eighty-five degrees most days. The temperature rarely drops below sixty. But that doesn't mean the climate never changes. There are three kinds of habitats on the Galapagos. A habitat is the natural home for different plants and animals.

On the islands, the coastal areas, near the water, are often rocky and bare. They are covered in solid lava fields, where not much will grow. This is called the coastal zone.

But hike a few miles inward, toward the center of the island, and the entire landscape changes. Giant cactuses grow in dry, rocky soil—a good food source for tortoises and iguanas. Thorny bushes and trees are everywhere. This is called the arid zone, which means it's like a desert. Everything is harsh and spiky. There is very little rain and no freshwater.

A few more miles inland, the land slopes upward toward the tops of the volcanoes. At a certain altitude—or height—rain begins to fall and misty clouds gather. The more rain there is, the more green plants can grow. This is called the moist uplands zone. Lush forests are filled with birds. Mosses, ferns, and other small green plants cover the ground.

At the very tops of some volcanoes are freshwater ponds or lakes. When the volcano is <u>dormant</u> or sleeping, the crater at the top—called the caldera—can fill with rainwater. It's a different world at the top of a Galapagos island than at the bottom—a wonderful place for birds to swim, with nothing but blue sky above them.

CHAPTER 5
The Weirdest Birds in the World

Birdwatchers from all over the world come to the Galapagos. There are more than eighty-five different kinds of birds to spot. Many of them are found nowhere else in the world! A species that can only be found in one place is called *endemic*.

Galapagos has some of the strangest, weirdest, and most interesting birds of any place on earth.

Perhaps the most famous bird in Galapagos is the blue-footed booby. Imagine a bird with bright blue webbed feet, like a duck, that waddles along, tilting from side to side. Boobies are large seabirds that fly out over the ocean and dive to catch fish. But on land, they are comically clumsy. They look like they might fall over at any moment.

When a male booby wants to get a female's attention, he lifts up his blue feet and shows them to her, over and over. He's showing her how blue they are! It turns out that having very blue feet is a good sign, for boobies. It means they're young and healthy. The males with the bluest feet will attract the most females at mating time.

Baby blue-footed boobies don't have blue feet. (Try saying that three times, fast!) Their feet don't turn blue until they are old enough to mate.

Boobies got their name from the Spanish word *bobo*, which means "fool" or "clown." The birds seem silly to humans, because they aren't afraid of anything. Like many of the birds on Galapagos, they don't run away when people approach.

But blue-footed boobies aren't the only boobies on the islands. There are red-footed boobies, too. Red-footed boobies are smaller. Their wingspan is only about three feet wide, while the blue-footed birds can have wingspans of nearly five feet. The red-footed boobies come in two colors—brown and white. Just picture a tall bird with red feet, a brown body, and a blue beak! It looks like someone had too much fun with a coloring book!

Red-footed booby

Perhaps most amazing of all is the flightless cormorant—and the name says it all. The bird can't fly! Why not? That was what Darwin wanted to know. His theory was that cormorants didn't need to fly, since there were no predators—other animals that hunted and ate birds—on these islands. So the cormorants had no reason to fly away to escape. And since they caught all their food by swimming and diving in the waters near shore, they didn't really need wings for flight. In fact, big wings just got in the way. They made it harder to dive. So, over time, the birds with smaller wings survived longer, and had babies with small wings. Over thousands of years, the wings of cormorants got smaller and smaller until they were no longer big enough for flight. The birds lost the ability to fly through evolution. The flightless cormorant is endemic to the Galapagos.

What other birds are endemic to the islands? The Galapagos penguin is one. It's a tiny penguin, only about nineteen inches tall—one of the smallest in the world. People often think penguins live only in cold climates, but that's not true.

No one is sure how the first penguins made their way to the Galapagos Islands, or why they

survived. But somehow it happened. Over time they have evolved into a new species of penguin that has adapted to live near the equator. They manage to stay cool in warm weather by diving into the sea. A very cold ocean current flows toward the islands, bringing lots of fish. It keeps the penguins well fed.

Another weird bird found on Galapagos is the magnificent frigatebird. The word *magnificent* is part of the bird's name, not just an opinion. They are huge—three and a half feet tall, with a wingspan of more than seven feet! Frigatebirds are more like living gliders. They can soar for days on the wind currents, rarely flapping their wings.

The most fascinating part of the frigatebird is
the red pouch under the male bird's throat. When
it's time to mate, the males puff up the red pouch,
like a huge red balloon! The idea is to attract the
females' attention, and it works. No one could
help but notice that bright red bulb, it's so big.

The largest bird on Galapagos is the waved albatross—a huge seabird with a wingspan of eight feet! Their wings have wavy lines in them—that's how they got the name. Like the frigatebird, these albatrosses can soar for hours or days. The tricky part for them is landing. They fly so well, it's hard for them to stop!

There are more than twelve thousand breeding pairs—one male, one female—of waved albatrosses on Española Island. But they don't live on the Galapagos year-round. They only come to the islands for six months, to mate and raise their babies. Then the whole family flies off to spend the rest of the year along the coasts of Ecuador and Peru. These huge birds always return to the Galapagos, though, to mate and raise their young.

How Species Reached the Galapagos

It's obvious how birds got to the Galapagos. They flew there. But what about plants and land animals? How did they arrive?

Plants arrived in several different ways. Seeds from plants may have stuck to a leaf or a small piece of wood that floated on the ocean until it reached the islands. A small plant, with the roots attached, might have arrived the same way. Or a bird may have eaten the seeds on the mainland and then flown to the Galapagos, where it pooped. Out came the seeds. In time, they took root.

Land animals, like tortoises and iguanas, are harder to explain. Did an iguana hitch a ride to the Galapagos on the back of a dolphin? Or did it get washed out to sea during a tidal wave? Did it float on the ocean waves and survive the six-hundred-mile journey?

If it was a female, already carrying eggs ready to be laid, it could have started a new population on the islands. The same could have happened with the giant tortoises. It would take only one female to arrive and lay her eggs to bring a new life-form to the islands.

CHAPTER 6
Land Animals in a Water World

The thing about islands is that they are surrounded by water. The ocean waters near the Galapagos are filled with dolphins, whales, sharks, and fish. It's a wonderful area to go snorkeling or scuba diving, because of the colorful tropical fish—nearly 450 different kinds! Some are found nowhere else. With bright white and yellow stripes, brilliant blue bodies, and glow-in-the-dark tails, these fish look as if they've been created for a Disney movie—but they're real.

There are many fewer whales than there were two hundred years ago. Still, they show up regularly, especially in the colder months. At least twenty-four different kinds of whales and dolphins can be seen near the Galapagos, including orcas and blue whales, the biggest animals alive today.

But the islands are also a great place for animals that like to spend time both on land and in the sea. Sea lions and fur seals are two species that live on the shore. Sea lions hang out on the rocks, cliffs,

and beaches of all the islands in huge numbers.

There are more sea lions than people on the islands—as many as fifty thousand altogether! They often sun themselves on the rocks, then cool off in the water as they hunt for sardines to eat. They are naturally curious and playful, and they don't shy away from people. But sometimes tourists forget that they are wild animals—big ones— weighing up to five hundred pounds. People have sometimes come too close and been bitten.

Fur seals have fur that keeps them warm, so they prefer the areas near shore, where the water is colder. During the pirate years, the fur seals were hunted for their pelts, which were sold all over the world for high prices. So many thousands were killed, the fur seals almost became extinct. Today, though, the fur seals are making a comeback.

Fur seal

Sea lions and fur seals are both mammals—animals that are born alive, not hatched from eggs, and drink their mothers' milk as

Rice rat

babies. They are two of only six mammals that are native to the Galapagos. The other four are dolphins, whales, bats, and rice rats.

Galapagos bottlenose dolphin

Another land animal that spends a lot of its time in the water is the Galapagos marine iguana. Most reptiles are land lovers, not water creatures. But in the Galapagos, some of the iguanas evolved in an unusual way. They learned to swim and dive! Why? There isn't much plant life on many of the islands—and there was probably even less a million years ago. So when the first iguanas arrived, it was probably difficult to find food. But by creeping into the ocean, they were able to find algae—a slimy water plant—to eat.

Many of the marine iguanas stick to the shallow waters in their search for food. But the larger males can actually dive from the rocks and plunge into the deep ocean. When they do this, however, they take in too much saltwater. To get rid of it, there is a special hole between their eyes. The iguanas blow hard, and the salt comes snorting out!

Marine iguanas have another special trait. They can shrink their own skeletons when food is scarce! Somehow, their bones actually get smaller, so they don't need as much food. Then, when the food supply is back to normal, their skeletons return to full size.

Some people think marine iguanas are ugly. Darwin thought so. He called them disgusting and clumsy. With their black bodies that match the black lava coastline, they make the rocky cliffs of the Galapagos look like they're crawling with something alive and unknown. There are more than two hundred thousand marine iguanas on the islands. Some areas are literally covered with them.

There are also land iguanas in the Galapagos. Some are bright yellow, and some of them are red. They munch on cactuses, chomping right into the sharp spines!

With all the fantastic birds, fish, mammals, and reptiles, it's no surprise that people want to visit this unspoiled part of the world.

But will visitors to the Galapagos ruin what nature has created?

CHAPTER 7
The Human Threat

People are the biggest threat to life in the Galapagos. Even the fiery volcanoes that erupt every so often can't do half the damage to these very special islands that humans can do.

The human threat started long ago. Pirates and whalers almost wiped out the tortoise population. Whalers put a big dent in the whale population and killed huge numbers of fur seals. Tiny birds like finches and pigeons were also killed by pirates, for sport. Early visitors could just hit them with a stick to kill them! The birds had no fear of people—they didn't know to fly away.

Hunting animals is only one way people have threatened the islands. Just as much damage—or even worse—was done when people brought new animals to Galapagos—ones that were not native to the islands.

Pigs, donkeys, and cats arrived on the islands, brought by humans for one reason or another. Unwanted rats arrived, too. They have always been stowaways on ships. Goats, however, have been the worst problem for more than two hundred years.

In the early 1800s, a sea captain let some goats from his ship graze on Santiago. Other sailors did the same thing. The goats escaped and kept reproducing, and in time the islands were overrun with them. They ate everything in sight—all the flowers, trees, shrubs, and bushes they could find. That left very little for the tortoises to eat.

Goats also destroyed the landscape in the moist uplands, where tortoises found shade and water. It wasn't long before the tortoises began to die out. Their food and habitats were gone.

By the 1990s, there were one hundred thousand goats living on Isabela Island. Santiago had eighty thousand goats destroying its landscape. Birds, insects, tortoises, and plants were all being affected. Something had to be done.

So in 1997, two organizations came up with a plan. They would hunt down and kill all the goats and pigs on the islands. It might sound harsh, but it was the only way to save the Galapagos from further damage. The two groups—Galapagos National Park Service and the Charles Darwin Foundation—raised millions of dollars to make the plan work. It was called Project Isabela.

The plan took years to succeed. The hunters were highly trained park wardens. They killed thousands of goats by shooting them from helicopters. But they couldn't find all of them. Goats are clever, good at hiding and escaping.

The park rangers knew that if they didn't get them all, the goats would breed again and the plan would fail.

So scientists came up with some tricks of their own. They sterilized a few goats, to make sure they couldn't have babies. Then they planted radio collars on them, so they could track the goats. These were called "Judas" goats—named for Judas in the Bible, who betrayed Jesus. When the Judas goats were put back on the islands, they led the hunters to the few remaining goats that hadn't been killed yet.

By 2006, all the goats, pigs, and donkeys on Santiago had been removed. Nearly all the goats on Isabela were removed, with only a few remaining. Those few are proving hard to catch!

But humans are still a major threat to the Galapagos. People sometimes bring food to the islands, and non-native insects might come along—hiding in fruits or vegetables. If those insects escape into the wild, they become part of the environment. They disturb the balance of life on the islands.

Also, even though it's against the law, fishermen still try to catch sharks, tuna, and sea cucumbers, which are prized as food in Asian countries. Sometimes people still try to take tortoises or rare birds to sell illegally in other parts of the world. Even tourists who love nature sometimes trample through landscapes.

The plants along the paths can be destroyed if too many people walk there. Tourists have left food on the beaches, at campsites. The food attracts animals and can be harmful to them. New and different foods may change their natural behavior.

Last but not least, the number of people living on the islands is growing. Five times as many people live there now as did in the 1970s. The number of tourists doubled and then tripled, too. Humans add to the pollution in many ways, and this could change the way the animals behave. Over time, the birds that are so fearless now may learn to fly away when humans approach. We would no longer be able to watch and observe how Galapagos animals behaved before humans arrived.

So scientists and nature lovers are always asking one big question: How can we make sure the Galapagos remain as unspoiled as possible in the future? How can we protect the species that would not exist if the islands weren't there?

In other words, how can we protect the Galapagos from ourselves?

CHAPTER 8
Protecting the Islands

When visitors arrive in the Galapagos today—at either the airport on Baltra or the one on San Cristóbal—as soon as they step off the plane, they pay $100. The money is the park entrance fee—nearly every square mile of the islands is part of Galapagos National Park. The money is used to protect this incredible, unusual part of the world.

The job of protecting the Galapagos belongs to the country of Ecuador and the Galapagos National Park. The national park was created in 1959 as a way of preserving the beautiful wildlife both on land and in the sea. Since then, strict rules have been set up for visitors.

First of all, many parts of the islands are

off-limits altogether. People could destroy the plants where native animals live just by walking through the area.

The rest of the park is divided up into official nature sites on various islands. There are seventy nature sites on land and seventy-nine water sites, for diving and snorkeling. But these sites can be visited only as part of a group, with a trained park ranger or guide. And the park puts strict limits on the number of people who can visit each site at any one time. Only sixteen people are allowed in each tour group. Only a few groups a day are permitted at each site. Each site has its own limit. Some scuba diving sites are so special that the park will allow only one group of sixteen at a time.

Most people who visit the Galapagos get off a plane and go immediately to a boat or ship. They live on the ship while touring for several days. Why? Some of the islands are a hundred

miles apart. The best way to see as many of them as possible is to travel by boat.

The national park has rules for the ships, too. There are only about eighty ships that are allowed

to bring visitors to the various nature sites. Most ships are small, carrying sixteen or fewer passengers. Even the routes the ships follow, from one island to another, are determined by the national park.

Some of the other rules are just common sense. People must stay at least six feet away from the animals. No riding the tortoises! No fishing is allowed, except on boats owned by local fishermen who live in the Galapagos. No walking off the paths. And the main rule, used in many national parks all over the world, is this: Take only pictures, leave only footprints. On the Galapagos, for example, that would mean resisting the urge to collect shells from the beach.

The entrance fees help to pay for nature guides who protect the park. But other organizations from around the world help, too. They raise money and suggest ways to protect the islands. Scientists who study plants, animals, and sea life are concerned about the Galapagos. The Charles Darwin Foundation built the research station on Santa Cruz. There is also a tortoise center nearby. That's where scientists study and breed giant tortoises. Now that the wild goats are gone, the scientists have been able to put tortoises back on islands where they were extinct or nearly extinct.

In fact, Galapagos is so important, it was named as a World Heritage Site by the United Nations. That means that many countries in the world all came together to agree that the Galapagos Islands are an important, extra-special place on earth—like the pyramids in Egypt or the Great Wall of China. They should be treasured, protected, and preserved.

What will happen in the future? Everyone agrees that these spectacular islands should be protected. But does that mean fewer people can visit? Should fewer people live there? Are there too many tourists already? What if someone wants to build a hotel or another airport? Should that be allowed?

Those are questions that have to be answered if we want to keep the blue-footed booby, the flightless cormorant, and the wonderful tortoises for future generations to see.

As many people have said, we love the Galapagos—but let's make sure we don't love the Galapagos to death.

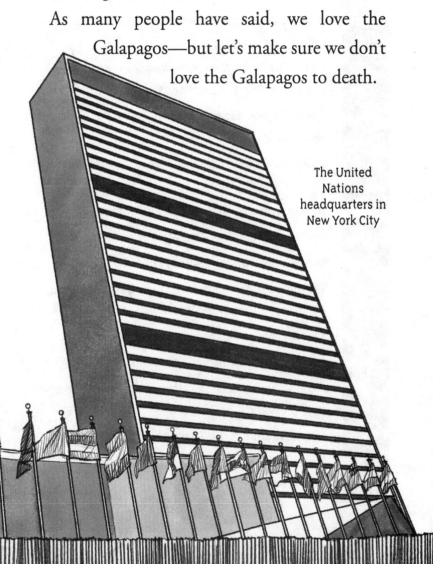

The United Nations headquarters in New York City

Timeline of the Galapagos Islands

1535	Discovered by Brother Tomas, the bishop of Panama
1680s	William Dampier and other pirates reach the islands
1790s	Whaling ships discover large numbers of whales in the waters near Galapagos
1825	Captain Benjamin Morrell, an American sea captain, sees a volcano erupting on the islands and later writes about it
1831	Charles Darwin departs for a trip around the world on the HMS *Beagle*
1832	Ecuador claims the Galapagos for its own and creates the first settlement
1835	Darwin arrives on the island of San Cristóbal, Galapagos
1841	Herman Melville visits Galapagos on a whaling ship
1859	Darwin's book *On the Origin of Species* is published
1942	The United States builds an air force base and runway on Galapagos during World War II
1959	Ecuador creates Galapagos National Park
1978	The Galapagos are named as a World Heritage Site
1997	Project Isabela begins, an attempt to eliminate all goats from the islands
2005	Largest volcano in the Galapagos erupts for eight days
2006	Project Isabela is declared a success after all goats have been removed

Timeline of the World

1492 — Christopher Columbus reaches the West Indies

1513 — Vasco Nunez de Balboa becomes the first European to see the Pacific Ocean

1522 — A Spanish ship becomes the first to sail around the world

1625 — New Amsterdam, later New York, is founded by the Dutch West India Company

1662 — Last known sighting of the dodo bird, and the species soon becomes extinct

1682 — Robert de La Salle explores the length of the Mississippi River and claims Louisiana for France

1751 — The first encyclopedia is published in France

1765 — James Watt invents the steam engine

1830 — Ecuador becomes an independent republic

1914 — Martha, the last passenger pigeon, dies in the Cincinnati Zoo

1937 — American aviator Amelia Earhart disappears somewhere in the Pacific on an around-the-world flight

1945 — The United Nations is founded

1976 — First outbreak of the Ebola virus

2003 — Space shuttle *Columbia* is destroyed on reentry

2010 — Deepwater Horizon oil spill, largest in US history, occurs in the Gulf of Mexico

Bibliography

*Books for young readers

*Hopkinson, Deborah. *Who Was Charles Darwin?* New York: Grosset & Dunlap, 2005.

Marris, Emma. "Goodbye Galapagos Goats." *Nature*. Published online January 27, 2009. http://www.nature.com/news/2009/090127/full/news.2009.61.html.

Nicholls, Henry. *The Galapagos*. New York: Basic Books, 2014.

Stewart, Paul D. *Galapagos: The Islands That Changed the World*. New Haven: Yale University Press, 2006.

Websites

www.galapagos.org
www.galapagosislands.com
www.galapagospark.org
www.seashepherd.org